BLUE-BLACK
IN LOVING MEMORY OF GARY TAYLOR JR.

BY SHERI PURPOSE HALL

PenFire Publishing

PenFire Publishing
Kansas City, MO penfirepublishing.com

Copyright ©2021 All rights reserved. No part of this book may be reproduced, scanned, or distributed in any printed or electronic form, including information storage and retrieval systems, without permission. Please do not participate in or encourage piracy of copyrighted materials in violation of the author's rights.
Please purchase only authorized editions.
First Edition: July 2021

ISBN: 978-1-952838-07-1
Library of Congress Control Number:
This book is a work of fiction. Names, characters, places, dates, and incidents are products of the author's imagination or are used fictitiously, satirically, or as parody. Any resemblance to actual persons, living or dead, business establishments, events, or locales is entirely coincidental.

10 9 8 7 7 5 4 3 3 1
Design, Layout, Edits: Sheri Hall & Brooke Hawkins

Dedication:

For my Little-Big cousin Gary Taylor.
You are the epitome of all things color and all things love.
Thank you.

My cousin
Sooooooo Black
He had Africa tatted on his chest

Sooooooo Black
He could code switch
Talk real crazy one minute
and be completely buttoned up the next

Sooooooo Black
He had dreams
That were still unfulfilled

Sooooooo Black
That he didn't get all the support
He was supposed to

Sooooooo Black
That he rocked RGB beads

Sooooooo Black
He equal parts hood,
collegiate dissertation,
and doctoral life lesson

My cousin
Sooooooo Black
He was blue

My cousin
Nipsey Hussel Black
Tookie Black
Marcus Garvey Black
Pan African Black
Wouldn't fight the power
Because he where the power at
Black

Where yo power at Black?

He
Arrogant Black
No time to be humble
We all gotta shine like
Vaseline
On patent leather shoes
Black

He
Vineyard Black
Know it all Black
Lemme give you this
This financial literacy
Enrich this community
Right quick
Black

He
Make improvements
On everything
He involved in
Black

Ain't no wardrobe
Without me Black
I make you look fly
Black
I stay fly
Black

So Black
I'm Blue-Black
Black

And ain't that beautiful?
To be unapologetic?
To not have been crushed by the world?
To climb the crack of the concrete and bloom?
Being Black boy joy and Blue radiating energy?

Have you ever seen
The color Blue smile
Peeking under a brim
Looking like majesty
And Light
The kind of Blue
That keeps you up at night
Doesn't let your eyes rest
Is a Grind Addict

Blue is the color of intelligence
The color of call out

Blue ain't always no baby
Blue grew up to be Royal

Blue was smart
But Blue don't comprehend
Lack of music
Lack of love
Lack of compassion

Blue don't comprehend
Excuses
Failure
Lack of discipline
Lack of motivation
Lack in general

Blue been grinding all his life
Blue be joyful
Blue be goofy
While carrying melancholy
Looking at the conditions
Of our people

Blue speaks truth
Blue operates in pure intention
Is trustworthy
Responsible
Honest
Loyal

Blue is stubborn
Blue say
If your community
Ain't built
As your body
Keep workin

Blue say
If your body ain't built
As your brain
Keep working

Blue say
If your finances
Ain't built as
Any of this
Keep working

Make a new business
Leave an inheritance
Blue got crazy work ethic
Blue got game
Blue got knowledge

Blue say
Know your price

Blue say
Know your worth

Blue say
Know the difference
Between the 2

Know the timeline
Know when to let it go
Keep those that rock
With you solid

Always be ready
Let's get it poppin
Let's go

Quit procrastinating
Be charitable
Recognize when you
Are being taken advantage of
Draw a line in the sand

Blue say
Help the fam
Include the fam

Blue say
Don't be afraid to be cocky
Be big

Take up space
Don't shrink for nobody

Blue say
You keep staying in this rut
Because everything was taken from us

Well
Take it back

Blue say
You are just as much
A part of the systemic oppression
If you sit back

Stand up
If you ready to take it back

Blue say
Stand up
If you ready to take it back

Say something
if you ready to take it back

Quit being silent
Scared
Poor and pitiful
Hold each other accountable

Blue be black enough
To know the fight
Ain't in the march
Or at the poll
But in the soul

In the business we create
And in what we take

So
Take it back
Take 18th and Vine back

Take the hood back
Take the community back
Take your family back
Take your health back

Quit saying the marathon continues
If you ain't ready to run it back

If you ain't ready to be
Blue-Black

www.ingramcontent.com/pod-product-compliance
Lightning Source LLC
Chambersburg PA
CBHW041327110526
44592CB00021B/2846

BLUE-BLACK

IN LOVING MEMORY OF GARY TAYLOR JR.

BY SHERI PURPOSE HALL

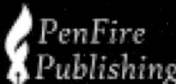

PenFire Publishing

$10.00
ISBN 978-1-952838-07-1
51000>